CLEANING SUCKS

Also by Rachel Hoffman
Unf*ck Your Habitat

CLEANING SUCKS

AN UNF*CK YOUR HABITAT GUIDED JOURNAL
FOR LESS MESS, LESS STRESS, AND
A HOME YOU DON'T HATE

✳ Rachel Hoffman ✳

ST. MARTIN'S GRIFFIN
NEW YORK

First published in the United States by St. Martin's Griffin, an imprint of
St. Martin's Publishing Group

CLEANING SUCKS. Copyright © 2019 by Rachel Hoffman. All rights reserved.
Printed in Turkey. For information, address St. Martin's Publishing Group,
120 Broadway, New York, NY 10271.

www.stmartins.com

Book design by Rita Sowins / Sowins Design
Illustrations by Shutterstock.com

The Library of Congress Cataloging-in-Publication Data is available upon request.

ISBN 978-1-250-21972-5 (trade paperback)

Our books may be purchased in bulk for promotional, educational, or business
use. Please contact your local bookseller or the Macmillan Corporate and
Premium Sales Department at 1-800-221-7945, extension 5442, or by email at
MacmillanSpecialMarkets@macmillan.com.

First Edition: January 2020

10 9 8 7 6 5 4 3

THIS JOURNAL BELONGS TO:

CONTENTS

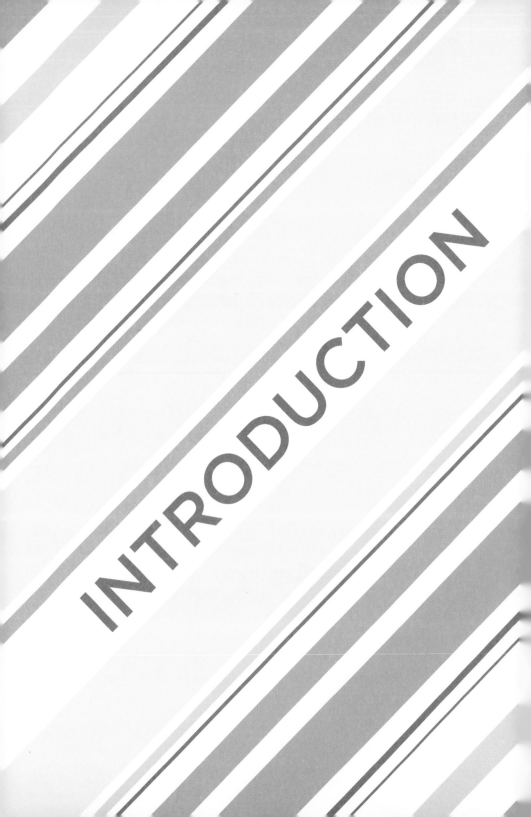

INTRODUCTION

When trying to get your mess under control, the "why" is just as important as the "how."

In this journal, you'll explore why your mess is the way it is, why you have trouble getting or keeping it under control, and what obstacles stand in your way, as well as how to work around or through them. When it comes to the "how," you'll find challenges, habit trackers, and much more to get you on track and keep you there. Whatever your habitat is—a house you own, an apartment you share, a room at your parents' place, a dorm room, or anywhere else—you can get it to a place where you're happy and comfortable.

As you work through this journal, you'll be adding skills and habits to your housekeeping toolbox, and at the same time, reexamining your relationship with cleaning and turning it into something healthier and more productive. And once you've spent some time working on those skills and habits, you'll probably find you feel less frustrated and overwhelmed by all those household tasks, and start seeing them as just a small detour in your day before you can get back to doing the things you actually enjoy.

It's important to understand that you can just start where you are. Even if you've tried countless things countless times, you still have a fresh chance to start again every single day. This is not a pass/fail class; it's a journey, and one that might not be easy or direct. You don't even have to work through this journal in order; jump around and see what strikes your fancy. The Unfuck Your Habitat (UfYH) system is based on the idea that any progress should be celebrated, and you don't have to do things in a certain order or within a certain amount of time to make lasting changes.

And remember, throughout your quest toward a clean home that you love, make sure to be kind to yourself. Sometimes you'll have setbacks and slow progress, but don't let that diminish your sense of accomplishment. It's very human to feel like a failure when you don't meet your goals right away, or to feel disappointed if you don't meet your own expectations, regardless of how lofty they may be. In working through this journal, you'll learn to reframe how you think about cleaning and redefine what success looks like for you. Housekeeping is a thankless, frustrating task that almost no one enjoys, but you can get to a point where it's not taking over your life. A few minutes a day of boring stuff you don't love to do is vastly better than days on end doing everything all at once.

Part of the UfYH system is understanding that all of this housekeeping and cleaning stuff is a continuous cycle, so there is always another chance to do it again, do it better, start fresh, or build on small successes. This is no "one and done" undertaking; it's a perpetual ebb and flow of triumph and defeat. Your goal should be less about perfection and more about improvement. Every small change for the better counts and can lead to bigger, better changes down the road.

If you've found that other housekeeping systems overwhelm or intimidate you, or that strict schedules and overly ambitious time investments just aren't realistic, rest assured that there is hope for you and your home. Changing your focus and your outlook toward cleaning can change your whole home. And you don't have to fully devote yourself to it; you can do a little at a time, when you can, and as long as you're consistently doing something—anything—you'll find that improvements will be happening around you, even if you're not completely consumed by it.

UfYH is about hope, about knowing that everyone, no matter their circumstances or situation, can transform their messy home into a place that's comfortable rather than stressful. It's about working within the limitations we all face, whether that's working or going to school full-time; living with disabilities, mental illness, chronic illness, or chronic pain; having grown up with an unhealthy relationship with cleaning; being on your own for the first time; or any of the million other things that can keep us from accomplishing what seems impossible. It *is* possible, and it's not nearly as hard as it seems.

TO
THINK
ABOUT

You might be tempted to jump right in and start cleaning.
You're motivated, you want to make changes, and that's great!
But before you get started, it's important to understand
why you feel the way you do about cleaning, what you'd like to
accomplish, and what's standing in your way.

- What do you want from your home?
- Why can't you get it?
- How can you get started?
- What do you do when life happens?

WHAT'S YOUR ENDGAME?

Listen, let's just get this out of the way: Cleaning is terrible and almost no one likes it. It can be hard to motivate yourself to do something you hate, especially if you feel like there's no payoff. So before you start, it's a good idea to know where you want to end up. Picture that all your hard work has paid off, and your home is in its ideal state. What does that look and feel like for you? Circle the words that fit best, and add your own.

✳ Bright	✳ Soft	✳ Organized
✳ Warm	✳ Sleek	✳ Quiet
✳ Cool	✳ Comforting	✳ Active
✳ Calm	✳ Minimal	✳ Serene
✳ Cozy	✳ Familiar	✳ Lively
✳ Spacious	✳ Inviting	✳ Tranquil

What's the first thing you want to do in your ideal home? Have friends over? Cook a big family dinner? Retreat to work on art? Sit and read your favorite book? Write about how you're going to want to use your space once you have it how you want it.

Wouldn't it be nice to
have people over?

HOW DOES
YOUR HOME
MAKE YOU FEEL?

It's no surprise that the state of your home can evoke strong emotions. Ideally, those emotions would all be positive, but realistically, they probably aren't. Figuring out how your environment makes you feel can help you learn how to make it better.

Check off the emotions that come to mind when you think of your home:

☐ Stressed out

☐ Angry

☐ Resentful

☐ Discouraged

☐ Depressed

☐ Anxious

☐ Guilty

☐ Frustrated

☐ ....

☐ ....

☐ ....

☐ ....

You matter enough to have a nice place to live.

How would you like it to make you feel?

- ☐ Calm
- ☐ Peaceful
- ☐ Accomplished
- ☐ Organized
- ☐ Happy
- ☐ Proud
- ☐ Content
- ☐ ....
- ☐ ....
- ☐ ....
- ☐ ....

I make no secret
of the fact that I would
rather lie on
a sofa than sweep
beneath it.

—SHIRLEY CONRAN, *SUPERWOMAN*

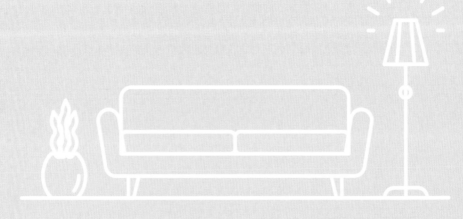

WHERE'S YOUR RETREAT SPACE?

Everyone should have at least one spot in their home where they can fully relax, renew, and forget that the rest of the world even exists. Do you have a space like that? If not, think about where you could create one. What might make a good retreat space?

If you could make your dream retreat space, what would you like it to be or to have? What kind of seating? Decor? What colors are you imagining? Are there plants, pictures, etc.?

ROADBLOCKS

Everyone has their own reasons why cleaning is difficult, whether those reasons are external or internal, physical, mental, or emotional. Think about what acts as a roadblock for you, preventing you from getting your mess under control. Once you identify *why* this is hard for you, you can start figuring out how to work with or around your roadblocks. Check off any of the reasons that apply to you, or list your own.

- [ ] Mental illness
- [ ] Disability
- [ ] Chronic illness/pain
- [ ] Learned to hate cleaning in childhood
- [ ] Don't know how
- [ ] Work/school full-time
- [ ] Live with someone who makes it difficult
- [ ] Just don't feel like it
- [ ] Doesn't feel worth it
- [ ] ....
- [ ] ....
- [ ] ....

As far as I'm concerned,
a house should look lived-in,
and I consider it clean
as long as I don't stick to it and
it doesn't give me cholera.

—JENNY LAWSON, *LET'S PRETEND THIS NEVER HAPPENED:
A MOSTLY TRUE MEMOIR*

FAILURE
IS A GIFT

Chances are, if you've picked up this journal, you've tried and failed to get your mess under control in the past. Maybe even a whole bunch of times. You might be feeling like a failure, and that's OK! But there's always an opportunity to learn from our failures, so let's try that before you get too down on yourself.

Think about what you've tried. Why do you think you didn't succeed with it?

....

What part(s) didn't work for you or your life?

....

Why did you ultimately give up?

....

Why did you start this journal?

....

Good news! No matter how many times you've tried, you can always start again, and with the right outlook, you *can't* fail because you can begin again whenever you want. Every day is a new opportunity for success. Feeling like a failure one day? The clock resets right away, and you have a fresh chance all over again.

It's not a failure,
it's an opportunity to try again.

It doesn't have to be perfect,
it just has to be better.

LETTING GO OF PERFECTIONISM

So many people avoid cleaning up because we feel like if we can't do it perfectly or completely, why bother doing it at all? That's totally understandable, but it's one of the reasons self-proclaimed perfectionists are often drowning in our own crap without ever getting it under control. Letting go of the idea that everything needs to be completely and perfectly done can be difficult, but embracing "good enough" instead of "perfect" can help you get started and get your mess under control, even if it's only a little bit at a time.

If you consider yourself a perfectionist, try setting a timer for five, ten, or twenty minutes and cleaning up what you can in that time. When the timer goes off, make yourself stop.

Once you've done this, look around. Does it look any better than it did when you started?

☐ Yes

☐ No

Try to keep working this way when you can. You'll eventually train yourself to let go of "perfect" and be content with "good enough."

Describe what you see.

....

....

....

WHAT ARE YOU HOLDING ON TO BECAUSE OF GUILT OR OTHER EMOTIONS?

Emotion can keep us hanging on to things we should have gotten rid of long ago. Whether it's sentiment because of the person associated with an item, or guilt about a gift we feel we need to keep forever, emotion can rule out decisions about what to keep and what to get rid of. Things don't have feelings, though, so really, you only need to worry about your own.

List a few things you'd get rid of if not for the emotion keeping you from doing so.

Gifts we don't really want can cause us a great deal of stress. For the most part, though, if the giver knows that you have received their gift and enjoy it (this part doesn't need to be true), you are not obligated to keep it forever. You can get rid of gifts. It's OK. They're yours now, and it's up to you to decide their fate.

If you don't love it,
you don't have to keep it.

START WHERE
YOU ARE

It's easy to be so overwhelmed by your mess that you feel like there's nowhere to start. And when you feel that way, chances are you're just not going to start at all, and that's not doing you any good. Guess what, though? You can start anytime, wherever you and your mess are.

Think of that one thing about your home that's stressing you out the most. You're probably going to be tempted to say, "Everything," but try to pick one thing that stands out a little more from everything else. (Dirty kitchen? Multiple months' worth of clothes to put away? A cluttered and unusable dining room table?)

Write it down here.

You're going to start there. Set a timer for twenty minutes and do what you can in that time.

When you're done, come back and record how you feel now that the first twenty minutes are done.

This is part of what I meant about housework. If it isn't important, what is? If it isn't done honorably, where is honor?

—URSULA K. LE GUIN, *VOICES*

REWARD PLANNING

Wouldn't it be great if we were all motivated to do things simply for the satisfaction of doing them? Unfortunately, it so rarely works that way. We're human, we like nice things, and we hate having to work hard if there isn't anything in it for us. Rewards are great and can take many different forms. When you think about how to reward yourself, don't just think about material things; also consider experiences that you enjoy. Rewards don't have to cost money or take a lot of effort; they can be as simple as taking a walk in nature or playing with a pet or relaxing with a video game.

What rewards—big or small, tangible or intangible—might motivate you to do some not-fun tasks?

....

....

....

....

....

....

Revisit this list as often as you need to. It's important to feel like your hard work is paying off, and aside from the feeling of accomplishment you'll have, a reward you enjoy is a great way to avoid feeling like all your work has been in vain.

SO YOU THINK YOU'RE BEYOND HELP

Sometimes it's all going to feel completely hopeless. You've tried so many times, and nothing seems to work. It's no surprise that feeling that way might lead you to believe that nothing will get better.

Some good news, though: No matter how bad it is, no matter how long you've been trying and failing to deal with your mess, it can get better. You can make it better. You're using this journal because you still want to succeed and you're willing to try again.

What's one tiny thing you can do right now? Don't think about the big picture—think about something that'll take just a minute and that won't take a lot out of you. Here are a few ideas if you can't come up with anything:

- Throw away some trash.
- Collect dishes from the room you're in.
- Put a few things away from the nearest flat surface.
- Wipe down a countertop.
- Put some dirty clothes in the hamper.
- Put a few pieces of clean clothes away.

What can you do that's quick and easy?

OK, now go do that. Once it's done, check in with how you're feeling. Does everything still feel hopeless?

☐ Yes

☐ No

If no, give it another shot with another tiny task.

And this mess is so big

And so deep and so tall,

We cannot pick it up.

There is no way at all!

—DR. SEUSS, *THE CAT IN THE HAT*

FEELING DISCOURAGED?

Sometimes it's difficult to celebrate our progress when we haven't accomplished as much as we'd like to. We tend to look at accomplishments as finish lines, not as checkpoints along the way. But this can prevent us from making progress.

Try reframing your perception of progress by keeping track of what you *have* done, as opposed to what you haven't. Instead of feeling discouraged at all the work left to do, let yourself be motivated by—and proud of—what you've completed.

List five home-related things you've accomplished recently, no matter how small. It counts even if it's just a part of a larger project; even if it seems insignificant.

1. ....

2. ....

3. ....

4. ....

5. ....

You can start over

again anytime.

SOMEONE IS DROPPING BY IN TWENTY MINUTES!

Do those words make you want to freak out a little bit? A lot? Is there swearing involved?

Be honest: How would you feel if you found out right now that an unannounced guest was en route to your home?

How long, realistically, do you think it would take to get your home guest-ready?

Do you think your guests deserve a better version of your home than the one you live in every day? Why or why not?

Think about the concept of "company-ready," and ask yourself what "you-ready" looks like. Would you want the everyday reality of your home to be a version in which anyone can stop by at any time?

Below, write down some small tasks you can do on especially bad days. Remember, every little bit counts! When you're having a low-energy day, revisit this list as needed.

REWARD YOURSELF!

Pick one thing from each column, do the not-fun thing first, and reward yourself with the more-fun one after.

NOT fun

* Clear off the nearest table/nightstand/etc.
* Wash dishes for a few minutes.
* Put away a few pieces of clothing.
* Throw away several pieces of trash.
* Put away a couple things within reach.
* Take a shower and change your clothes.

MORE fun!

✳ Listen to a song you love.
✳ Watch a TV show/listen to a podcast.
✳ Go outside for a few minutes.
✳ Eat or drink something delicious.
✳ Read a chapter in a good book.
✳ Play a game (video/app/etc.) that you enjoy.

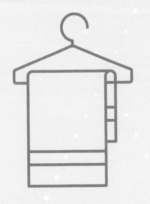

You're better than your mess.

CLEANING
ANXIETY

For many people, cleaning can trigger or exacerbate anxiety, sending intrusive or anxious thoughts spiraling out of control and preventing you from making significant progress. It's important to find a balance between getting tasks done and maintaining your mental health.

If you're feeling anxious about cleaning up, try looking away from the big picture and focusing on a small task instead. Set some clear boundaries about what you're going to work on and what time frame you're working with.

What's one small task you can start and complete within twenty minutes?

Start your timer and work on that task.

Once you're done, check in with how you're feeling. Overall, how are you feeling after those twenty minutes?

Making significant changes in your environment can induce or worsen anxiety, so make sure you check in frequently to see if you're feeling OK. If you get to a point where your anxiety is making it tough to keep going, it's perfectly fine to stop for a while and pick it up again when you're feeling a little more settled.

You deserve a
nice home.

EXCUSE OR REASON?

We all have justifications for why we don't clean, and we've mostly been conditioned to think of them as excuses. But if you're living with a physical or mental illness, it's important to understand the difference between excuses and reasons. Think about why you don't clean and, on the next page, write down a few things that come to mind.

Now, consider the following for each of those things: Does it explain why you *don't want to* do it, or does it explain why you *can't* do it? That's the difference between an excuse and a reason. Check off whether each thing is a reason or an excuse. If your justifications are reasons, don't beat yourself up about it. If they're excuses, well, that gives you a place to start when it comes to making changes.

There's a lot of judgment wrapped up in keeping a clean home. If you have reasons why you can't, instead of excuses why you don't want to, try not to turn that judgment inward. Instead, brainstorm how you can still accomplish the things that you need to within the framework of what your illness allows.

	Reason	Excuse
....	☐	☐
....	☐	☐
....	☐	☐
....	☐	☐
....	☐	☐
....	☐	☐
....	☐	☐
....	☐	☐
....	☐	☐

You are capable of

great things.

LEARNING THE BASICS

Here's where you'll discover tools for:

- Building your systems
- Necessary habits
- Big projects

Now that you understand the "why," let's get started on the "how." Many people get overwhelmed trying to get a handle on how to clean, and many never really learned how. Getting a grip on the basics will make getting your mess under control a much easier project.

20/10s

20/10: Twenty minutes of cleaning followed by a ten-minute break.

When you think about cleaning, you probably picture an intense day- or weekend-long top-to-bottom marathon session. No wonder you don't want to clean—that sucks! Having to devote an entire day or weekend to something that almost no one enjoys is enough to put you off of it forever. But you can still get your chaos under control without losing an entire day or weekend to it!

One of the goals of this journal is to get you to reframe how you look at cleaning. Enter the 20/10: twenty minutes of cleaning followed by a ten-minute break. Tackling your mess in small chunks with breaks in between will help keep you from feeling overwhelmed and will also allow you to get back to doing something way more fun than cleaning your home.

Set a timer for twenty minutes and work on whatever mess is closest at hand.
Once the timer goes off, stop cleaning and take a ten-minute break.

What did you get accomplished in your twenty minutes?

....

....

What did you do during your ten-minute break?

....

Give yourself
permission to stop.

TWENTY-MINUTE SPRINTS

Now that you've got the concept of a 20/10 down, let's look at how you can use them to get ahead of your mess and get what's already there under control. You don't need to devote an entire day to cleaning. In fact, it's better if you don't. Instead, try to devote just twenty minutes at a time a few times a day (if you can) to picking up, cleaning up, and working on around-the-house projects.

Below, list some tasks that you can do in twenty minutes. Then, pick one thing from that list, do it, and spend a little while feeling comfortably smug about getting it done.

1. ....

2. ....

3. ....

4. ....

5. ....

6. ....

7. ....

8. ....

9. ....

10. ....

I did not want my
tombstone to read,
"She kept a really clean house."

—ANN RICHARDS,
HIGH HEELS AND BACKWARDS

BREAKS

Since the ten-minute break is so important, brainstorm a few things you can do with that time. Taking a little time to do something you enjoy can keep you motivated, or at least keep you from hating the cleaning process more than necessary.

Below are some suggestions. Add your own ideas that'll give you a few minutes off from kicking your mess's ass.

- Have a snack.
- Catch up on your social media.
- Work on a crossword puzzle.
- Take a short walk.
- Play with your pet.
- Have a little dance party with yourself (or with anyone else around, including your pet).
- Make a cup of tea or coffee (or your beverage of choice).
- Call or text a friend or family member.

[Her] version of cleanliness was
next to godliness, which
was to say it was erratic,
past all understanding, and
was seldom seen.

—TERRY PRATCHETT, *UNSEEN ACADEMICALS*

CLEANING
IS A CYCLE

As much as we'd love to clean something once and be done with it forever, it just doesn't work that way. Which, let's be honest, sucks. Like, a lot. If you live in your home and use the things in it, you're going to need to clean up regularly. Keeping a clean home is a continuous cycle, as much as we all wish it weren't so. But if you have a realistic idea of how often you should repeat certain tasks, you can figure out a cleaning schedule that will work for your life.

Below, list some of your most common tasks and how often you should do them. Here's a few to get you started.

Task	Ideal Frequency
Dishes	
Laundry	
Wash bedsheets	
Clean bathroom	

Few tasks are more like
the torture of Sisyphus than
housework, with its endless
repetition: the clean becomes
soiled, the soiled is made clean,
over and over, day after day.

—SIMONE DE BEAUVOIR

WASH, DRY, AND PUT IT AWAY, DAMMIT!

Laundry and dishes have three steps. We tend to forget about (or, honestly, choose to ignore) the third step, leaving clean clothes and clean dishes languishing, taking up space and contributing to the clutter, instead of putting them away.

Today, when you do your dishes or laundry, plan to give yourself a reward once all steps are complete.

What will your reward be?

....

....

....

....

Check off when you complete each step:

    ——   1. Wash

    ——   2. Dry

    ——   3. Put it away, dammit!

Excuses
are
boring.

MAKE
YOUR BED!

Wait! Don't turn the page yet! I know you hate making your bed. I know you don't see the point, but hear me out.

If you hate making your bed, take a minute to think about why. Which of these apply?

☐ It was a punishment/I hated doing it growing up.

☐ I don't see the point.

☐ I believe an unmade bed allows the mattress to "air out."*

☐ It takes too long.

☐ No one else is going to see it.

A messy bed makes the whole room look messier and invites more chaos (laundry piling up, dirty sheets, etc.). Taking a minute or less to pull the sheets up and straighten the blankets and pillows gives you a little bit of order and helps you establish habits that'll influence the rest of your home.

* Think about rumpled piles of bedding on an unmade bed and really consider whether that increases airflow to the mattress. Spoiler: It doesn't. The best prevention for dust mites is washing your bedding regularly and vacuuming your mattress periodically.

Try making your bed every day for a week. Check off each day once it's done. If you're someone who thinks it takes too long, time yourself to see how long it actually takes.

		How Long Did It Take?
Day 1	☐	
Day 2	☐	
Day 3	☐	
Day 4	☐	
Day 5	☐	
Day 6	☐	
Day 7	☐	

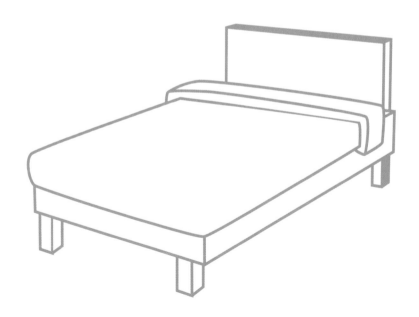

SINK
ZERO

Dishes are the worst. Do you ever feel like you're really finished with them? As soon as they're washed, we make more, and it feels like we'll never catch up. It hardly seems fair, but that's how dishes work, unfortunately. However, there is a way to avoid feeling like you're drowning in dirty dishes.

Once a day, aim to hit Sink Zero, when all of your dishes are dealt with, either handwashed or put in the dishwasher. It may be for just a fleeting moment, but that's OK! One minute when you're totally caught up on your dishes is better than never getting there at all.

Every day for a week, record the time that you hit Sink Zero. Missed a day? Don't worry—tomorrow is a brand-new chance to hit Sink Zero.

Day	Time I Got to Sink Zero

Those dishes aren't going
to wash themselves!

It's OK to
hate it,
but you still
have to do it.

UNFUCK
TOMORROW MORNING

Are your mornings pure chaos, with you scrambling to get everything together in a few scant minutes before you fly out the door, stressed out and almost definitely forgetting something? Give Tomorrow You a gift by unfucking your morning the night before, and watch how much easier your mornings can get.

- ☐ Wash the dishes in your sink.
- ☐ Get your outfit for tomorrow together.
- ☐ Set up coffee/tea/breakfast.
- ☐ Make your lunch.
- ☐ Put your keys somewhere obvious.
- ☐ Take your meds/set them out for tomorrow.
- ☐ Charge your electronics.
- ☐ Put a little cleaner in the toilet bowl.
- ☐ Set your alarm.
- ☐ Go to bed at a reasonable hour.
- ☐ ....
- ☐ ....
- ☐ ....

If you find yourself overwhelmed in the morning, a little bit of effort tonight can keep you on track for a calm, easy start to your day tomorrow.

DO ONE THING EVERY TIME YOU LEAVE OR ENTER A ROOM

A great way to keep from drowning in your own crap is to try to do something to improve a room each time you enter or leave it. It can be something very small, like putting one or two items away, or something a bit more involved, like wiping down a counter.

Label the rooms in your home and list what you could do in each one.

Room	Task

With enough repetition, these little tasks will turn into regular habits and will give you the chance to get ahead of your mess before it gets ahead of you.

Every little bit
counts.

KEEP YOUR
FLAT SURFACES
CLEAR

Flat surfaces tend to accumulate a lot of junk. Cluttered counters, tables, and other flat surfaces can make your whole environment look a lot messier, but cleaning them up can make everything seem a whole lot cleaner right away.

What's your messiest flat surface?

Go ahead and clear it off. Give yourself a big ol' check mark once that's done.

Do it now;
don't leave it for
later.

Now, challenge yourself to keep it clear every day for a week. Check off each day once it's done. If you didn't get it done one day (or two, or more . . .), jot down why.

Day 1	☐	
Day 2	☐	
Day 3	☐	
Day 4	☐	
Day 5	☐	
Day 6	☐	
Day 7	☐	

USE YOUR WAITING TIME WISELY

Every day, we end up doing a lot of waiting around, and those short little amounts of waiting time can be used productively. For example, if you need to wait for your coffee to brew, you can use those few minutes to wipe down countertops or wash some dishes.

Think about times during your day that you need to wait for a few minutes or more (waiting for the shower to heat up, dinner cooking in the oven, etc.). Then, come up with a few ideas of what you can do with that time.

Small changes make a huge difference.

Waiting For	Can Do While Waiting

DO SOMETHING
EVERY DAY

Even on your busiest days, doing just a little bit will make a big difference. You may not have more than a few minutes to devote to cleaning up, but anything you can do will make a difference and keep you in the habit of actually doing something. For one week, keep track of something around the house that you manage to get done each day, no matter how small it seems.

Day 1 ....

Day 2 ....

Day 3 ....

Day 4 ....

Day 5 ....

Day 6 ....

Day 7 ....

You don't have
to do much; you just have
to do something.

Move slowly,
but move forward.

GET IN THE HABIT

In order to get something done every day, you may need to schedule it into your day, even if it's just mentally. For example, some people like to do not-favorite tasks like cleaning first thing in the morning so it's over and done with and they don't have to worry about it for the rest of the day. Some people find they're more productive right at the end of a work or school day, before they change clothes and change gears into relaxation mode.

Where in your day do you think you can find twenty minutes to devote to cleaning up?

The internet will still be there in twenty minutes!

Every day for a week, try doing something during that twenty-minute window. Write down what you got done, or if you didn't manage it, write down what prevented you from doing it.

Day 1	
Day 2	
Day 3	
Day 4	
Day 5	
Day 6	
Day 7	

Time to go be
a badass.

INVISIBLE CORNERS

Invisible corner: Any pile or accumulation of household crap that's been there so long that it no longer registers when you look around.

- The pile on the end of the kitchen counter
- All that stuff on the chair in the bedroom
- Those random boxes in the corner of the living room
- That shelf that keeps collecting stuff

Invisible corners have become such a part of the landscape that you've probably forgotten they need to be dealt with. But even though you might not consciously see them, they're still there and they still need to be cleaned up.

Identify one invisible corner.

Set a timer for twenty minutes and work on getting every one of the items in that invisible corner back where it belongs. Check off when those twenty minutes have passed.

If twenty minutes isn't enough, take a ten-minute break and repeat until the invisible corner is vanquished.

Look around. What are some other invisible corners you can deal with?

_____

_____

_____

_____

_____

_____

_____

Your stuff is hiding in plain sight.

SOLVING
STORAGE

One of the most common contributors to messy spaces is a lack of storage, or an impractical storage space. Once you get your storage under control, keeping the mess to a minimum will get a whole hell of a lot easier.

To determine the best place to store items that currently don't have a home, ask yourself the following questions:

- How often do I use this item?
- Where do I use it?
- Is there somewhere logical to store it that's near where I use it?
- If not, can I create a logical place to put it?

If your storage space is convenient, you're more likely to put things away because it's easy. Keep that in mind and make sure your infrequently used items aren't taking up precious, easily accessed storage space that could be used for more frequently used things.

Imagine the box on the next page is an empty storage space in your home. Fill it (neatly!) with items that need a new home.

RULE
OF FIVE

There will be days when your time is in short supply, and you can't even carve out enough for a 20/10. Maybe you think you can't make a difference without investing a lot of time, but you might be surprised at what you can get accomplished in almost no time at all. Below are some ideas for five things you can do in five minutes or less:

1. Throw away five pieces of trash.

2. Wash five dishes.

3. Put away five items of clothing.

4. Do a five-minute cleaning blitz in any room.

5. Find five things that aren't where they belong and put them away.

What are five more things you can do quickly? List them here.

1. ....

2. ....

3. ....

4. ....

5. ....

Housekeeping
ain't no joke.

—LOUISA MAY ALCOTT, *LITTLE WOMEN*

NAME THE THING
THAT SCARES YOU

It's not always just the everyday tasks that stop us in our tracks. We all have something big and intimidating that we know we need to work on, but we can't wrap our heads around the task to get started.

What task or project is most overwhelming to you right now?

How do you feel when you think about starting it?

How do you think you'll feel once it's done?

This is your Big Project, and you're going to conquer it! Give your Big Project a name. (You can swear. We won't tell anyone.) Write it in the banner at the top of this page.

You can nap when
you're done.

HOW DO YOU EAT AN ELEPHANT?

One bite at a time! How do you tackle a Big Project? The very same way. A Big Project is really just a series of Little Projects, and Little Projects are easy! Well, they're easy-ish. Easier, at least.

What are the first three steps you need to get started on that overwhelming task? Be specific, and make those three steps as small as you can. For example: Gather your supplies together, or collect all the trash or dishes, or start one load of laundry.

1. ....

2. ....

3. ....

Now that you have your first steps identified, go do step 1.

FIRST CHECK-IN:

* How long did it take? ....

* How do you feel now? ....

* Does the task still feel intimidating? ☐ Yes ☐ No

Now move on to step 2. After you've done your first twenty minutes of work, check back in. How does it feel to finally get going on your Big Project?

SECOND CHECK-IN:

* What did you get done?
* What do you need to do next?
* How are you feeling about your project now?

Continue working twenty minutes at a time, taking a ten-minute break in between, until the project is done. This may take days or even weeks, depending on the scope of the project, but you're going to use the same 20/10 method throughout until it's complete.

CHALLENGES

Now that you have the basics down, it's time to put them into practice. The following challenges will help you turn those basics into habits while making real progress in the meantime.

- Mini-challenges
- Keeping it up
- Unfuck your weekend

MINI-CHALLENGES

Only have a few minutes to spare? Try one of the mini-challenges on the following pages. They don't take a lot of time, but when added up, they'll make a big difference. Set a timer for five or ten minutes and do what you can before the timer goes off. You might not get everything done, but you'll make a dent!

Get shit done.

MINI-CHALLENGES

- Pick one shelf or surface that's cluttered or dirty, and clean it off.
- Collect any trash or dishes from the room you're in. Wash the dishes and properly dispose of the trash.
- Make your bed. Pull up the bedding, straighten the pillows, and tuck everything in to look neat, if you're feeling fancy.
- Clean the microwave or stovetop (or both).
- Put away everything around your front door or entrance to your home (shoes, jackets, bags, etc.).
- Change out your hand and dish towels for clean ones.
- Put away clean laundry or dishes.
- Dust a few surfaces of the room you're in. Don't forget to look up in the corners and down to the baseboards, where dust can accumulate but rarely gets dealt with.
- Wipe down door handles, faucets, and light switches. Germs, grime, and dirt love to hang out there.
- Sweep/vacuum/mop the floor of one room. Get in all the corners, and underneath whatever you can get to.
- Look around, find ten things that aren't where they belong, and put them away.
- Collect all your trash and recycling and take it out.
- Clean out your wallet/purse/book bag.
- Clean and organize one shelf of your fridge or pantry. Get rid of anything expired or spoiled.

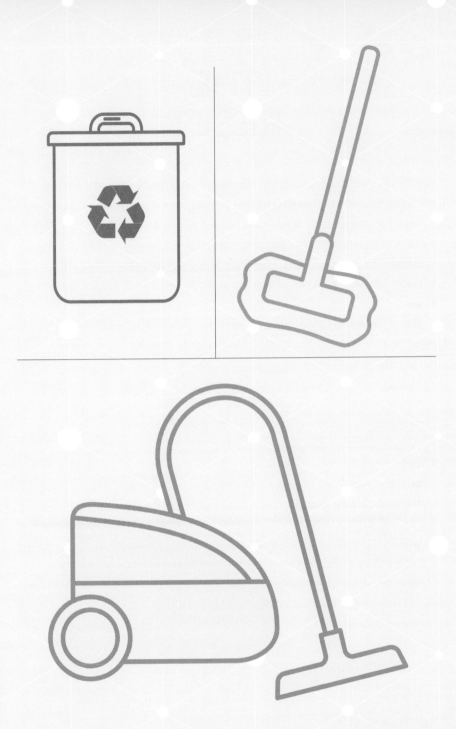

THE
RESET

Once you've tackled a space and cleaned it up, you're going to want to keep it that clean forever. Which is great, but it doesn't just magically happen. It requires a little effort on your part, which is sort of annoying but fortunately not too difficult.

Behold the reset. Each day, spend just a few minutes getting that space back to clean. A few minutes each day will prevent the need for a massive cleanup all at once.

Pick a space that tends to get cluttered and overwhelming and identify it here.

Working twenty minutes at a time, clear it off and clean it up.

How long did it take in total?

Now, every day for a week, reset that space back to clean. On the next page, record how long it takes each day.

Day 1 ....

Day 2 ....

Day 3 ....

Day 4 ....

Day 5 ....

Day 6 ....

Day 7 ....

Don't put it down, put it away.

TAKE A PICTURE, IT'LL LAST LONGER

Sometimes, when you're in the middle of cleaning, it's difficult to see the progress you've made. If you're making incremental changes, you tend not to notice them, which can be really frustrating. Having photographic proof of where you started to compare to where you are now helps you see how much of a dent you've made. It also gives you a reminder of what a room or an area can look like when it's clean, which can be helpful when you feel like things are never going to get better again.

What's the room or area that's stressing you out the most?

Take a picture of it as it is now and stick it here, or draw your best artist's rendition.

This is your "before."

How do you feel when you look at this picture? (It's OK if your answer is just a string of profanities.)

Do twenty minutes of work on this area and take another picture.

Can you see the progress you've made? ☐ Yes ☐ No

How do you feel about it now?

Continue working on it twenty minutes at a time, taking a ten-minute break in between, and keep documenting your progress with pictures.

UNFUCK YOUR WEEKEND

As much as we try to avoid marathon cleaning, the truth of the matter is that sometimes you need to fit the bulk of your cleaning into the short time you have off from Real Life™. That's where Unfuck Your Weekend comes in! Each day only requires a few hours' worth of work, leaving you with your freedom the rest of the day. If you don't have an actual weekend, it's completely fine to do these challenges over the course of two random days. Whatever works for you and your life!

On the next pages are sets of challenges for each day of your weekend. Do what you can for each challenge in twenty minutes, then take a ten-minute break after each one. You can take more time if you need, but make sure it's a set amount of time, and that you're taking breaks in between. It might not be perfect when you're done, but it'll be much better!

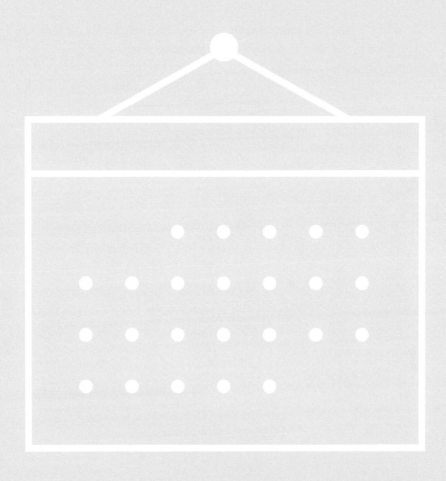

DAY 1

CHALLENGE 1: GETTING STARTED

We're going to start with something fairly easy for your first twenty minutes. Do what you can in that time, and if part of the challenge doesn't apply to you, find something similar to do during that time.

- ☐ Get out of bed!
- ☐ If you have immediate access to a washing machine, strip your bedding and start a load of laundry.
- ☐ If you don't, make your bed.
- ☐ Round out your twenty minutes by doing some dishes or loading (or emptying and reloading) your dishwasher.

Not sure what to do with your ten-minute break? Use this space to jot down your thoughts on this challenge. Did you get everything done, or did you skip a step or two? Did you do something else instead? How do you feel with your first challenge completed?

CHALLENGE 2: TO THE KITCHEN!

This twenty minutes, head to the kitchen for some basic cleaning and maintenance.

- ☐ Clear items off countertops and wipe the counters down.
- ☐ Clean off the stovetop.
- ☐ Look around for any out-of-place items or messes that need to be dealt with and deal with them.
- ☐ Continue washing dishes if necessary for the rest of your twenty minutes.

How did you do with this challenge?

....

....

....

....

....

....

....

....

CHALLENGE 3: BATHROOM BREAK!

We're headed to the bathroom next for a basic wipe down and surface clean.

- ☐ First, if you threw laundry in during Challenge 1, check if it's ready for the dryer.
- ☐ Fill the tub and sink with hot water and cleaner.
- ☐ Pour a little cleaner in the toilet bowl.
- ☐ Wipe down all surfaces.
- ☐ Put things away if they aren't in their homes.
- ☐ Empty the trash.
- ☐ Sweep the floor.
- ☐ Scrub the toilet and wipe down the seat and surfaces.
- ☐ Finally, drain the sink and tub and wipe them down.

Do you feel like you got a fair amount accomplished in twenty minutes, or did this challenge take longer? What are some things you can do on a daily basis to make your bathroom cleaning go faster?

....

....

....

....

....

....

CHALLENGE 4: CONQUERING THE FLOORDROBE

Head to the bedroom for your next twenty minutes, where you'll deal with your laundry, both clean and dirty. If you have a floordrobe (or chairdrobe, or bedrobe), now is the time to reintroduce your clothes to the closet or dresser.

- ☐ Collect dirty laundry and put it in the appropriate receptacle.
- ☐ Put away shoes, bags, and other accessories that aren't where they belong.
- ☐ Put away clean laundry that's in baskets, on furniture, or strewn across the floor.

Did you have too much laundry to fully deal with in twenty minutes? What ideas do you have to make putting laundry away less of an ordeal?

CHALLENGE 5: BACK TO THE BEDROOM

For this twenty minutes, focus on your bedroom's flat surfaces.

☐ Clear off your dresser.

☐ Put away or straighten up all the items on your nightstand.

☐ Clear and straighten any shelves.

☐ Give all those flat surfaces a good dusting.

How are you feeling about your bedroom after spending two twenty-minute challenges in it?

CHALLENGE 6: LAUNDRY OR FREESTYLE CHALLENGE

Now it's time to deal with your laundry area, if you have one. If you don't, you can revisit an earlier challenge you didn't get to complete.

If you have a laundry room/area:

☐ If you have a load of laundry in, check if it's dry yet. If so, remake your bed.

☐ In your laundry area, put away items on top of machines or that are out of place.

☐ Wipe down the washer and dryer.

☐ Empty the lint trap.

☐ Sweep the laundry area.

If you don't have a laundry room/area:

Spend twenty minutes cleaning up anything from an earlier challenge that you didn't get to. Jot down what you're working on:

....

....

....

....

....

....

CHALLENGE 7: LIVING IT UP

Head to the living room/family/common area for this challenge.

☐ Clear off and wipe down any tables.

☐ Straighten the bookshelves and put away anything that isn't where it belongs.

☐ Pick up items on the floor and put them away.

☐ Fold blankets and reset and fluff pillows.

☐ Dust what needs dusting.

What are some words that come to mind about this common area now that it's clean(er)? How do you feel about spending time here?

CHALLENGE 8: YOU CAN'T AVOID IT FOREVER

If you've been relieved that none of the challenges have made you deal with something you've been avoiding, that's what you're going to work on for this twenty minutes. Invisible corner, junk drawer: Whatever it is you don't want to deal with, go deal with it.

What are you going to work on for this challenge?

Check here when you're done.

How do you feel at the end of Day 1?

Once you're done, take the rest of the day off and come back tomorrow morning for Day 2!

DAY 2

Welcome to Day 2! Just a little bit more work and then you're free to enjoy the rest of your day! Don't forget about your breaks in between each challenge.

CHALLENGE 1: FLAT SURFACES

This twenty-minute session you're going to spend a little more time on the various flat surfaces in your home.

- ☐ Start by making your bed.
- ☐ Find a flat surface (counter, shelf, table, etc.) that hasn't been cleaned off yet. Put all misplaced items away, straighten the remaining items, and wipe down or dust the space.
- ☐ Repeat with other flat surfaces for the rest of the twenty minutes.

How many surfaces did you get to during this challenge? If you still have more to go, write down what they are here so you can revisit them later.

....

....

....

....

....

....

CHALLENGE 2: FLOOR ROUTINE

For this challenge, you're going to sweep, vacuum, or mop whatever floors you have time to get to. If you did all the Day 1 challenges, your floors should be mostly clear and ready to be cleaned.

List which rooms have floors that need to be cleaned, and check off once you've done each room.

- [ ] ....
- [ ] ....
- [ ] ....
- [ ] ....
- [ ] ....
- [ ] ....
- [ ] ....
- [ ] ....

If you didn't get to every room, make note of which rooms are left for the next time you do this challenge. Or, if you're feeling motivated, take another twenty minutes and do some more.

CHALLENGE 3: REDUCE, REPLACE, REFILL

This challenge can happen in either the kitchen or the bathroom, depending on what needs more time.

- ☐ Go through and get rid of expired items.
- ☐ Find a few weird nooks or crannies to clean, like behind, under, or next to appliances or fixtures.
- ☐ Replace towels and sponges.
- ☐ Replace or refill things like toilet paper, paper towels, soap, etc.

If you need to stock up on anything, make a little list here to remind yourself.

CHALLENGE 4: ANIMAL STYLE

If you have pets, you'll spend this challenge on their stuff. Pet-free? Use this twenty-minute session to finish up anything unfinished from another challenge.

- ☐ Wash food and water bowls.
- ☐ Clean the litter box, if applicable.
- ☐ Wipe down the eating area.
- ☐ Collect toys and put them away.
- ☐ Check if pet bedding needs to be washed. (If you can't remember when it was last washed, it probably stinks.)

No pets? What did you get done during this challenge?

CHALLENGE 5: PAPER PUSHER

Everyday life involves a lot of paperwork. During this challenge, you'll deal with your mail, bills, and other paperwork.

- ☐ Shred or recycle mail as needed.
- ☐ Pay any bills that are due.
- ☐ Set up automatic bill pay if you can.
- ☐ Recycle or file bills once you've paid them.

What can you do to stem the flow of paperwork you have to deal with? Think about some ways to keep paper from coming into your home, or for dealing with it once it's there.

CHALLENGE 6: THE FINISH LINE

You're almost there! Time for one final lap around your home.

- ☐ Starting in one room, find one thing that didn't get done yet and do it.
- ☐ Repeat in each room.
- ☐ Give germy surfaces a wipe down. This includes door handles, light switches, faucets, and knobs.

How do you feel after two days of challenges? What are some words that come to mind about how your home feels now? Was there something you really hated doing, or some tasks that weren't as bad as you thought they'd be?

_____

_____

_____

_____

_____

_____

That's it! You're done! Enjoy your clean(er) home and the rest of your weekend!

SHARING SPACE

When you live with other people, keeping the mess under
control gets a little more complicated. Just because you're committed
to cleaning up doesn't mean everyone else in your household is.
Use the tools in this section to navigate difficult conversations and
find your way to fairly divided chores and tasks.

- Useful conversations
  - Fair chore charts

HAVE USEFUL CONVERSATIONS

Getting your mess under control gets way more complicated when you share your space with others. Communication is the key to keep you all sane, happy, and not at each other's throats.

Need to address something about your home with someone you live with? Use this template to start the conversation. And remember to go into the conversation without anger, resentment, or frustration. Allowing those negative emotions to color your conversation from the get-go will almost definitely ensure that the discussion isn't going to go anywhere good.

What issue needs to be addressed?

....

Have you discussed this issue before? ☐ Yes ☐ No

When was the last time you discussed it? (Not fought about it; discussed it.)

....

Why are you frustrated by it?

....

Do you know how the other person feels about it?

....

If so, what's their take on it?

....

What steps can be taken toward a resolution?

....

What does the timeline for change look like?

....

When should you revisit the topic?

....

During your conversation, keep the following in mind:
- Are you avoiding defensiveness, resentment, and aggression?
- Are you both trying to understand each other's point of view?
- Is each person being given time to speak and be heard?
- Are you trying to work toward a resolution instead of airing grievances?

RESENTMENT

When you share space with someone and you're making a valiant effort at cleaning up, chances are they aren't going to be on the same page as you. Hell, they might not even be reading the same book.

Instead of getting angry or resentful, remember that your cohabiter is not the enemy. Really. And unless you live with a real jerk, they're not actively trying to sabotage you. They just have different priorities than you do. So when you're interacting with someone who's not pulling their weight like you think they should, keep in mind that almost no one is going to come around to a point of view coming at them with rage and resentment.

Here are a few honest questions to ask yourself if you're feeling resentful of the person or people you live with:

- Have I made my point of view clear, without anger or frustration, or has every "conversation" about it been the lead-in to a fight?
- How strict are my standards for what I want done?
- Has the person tried to contribute in the past but been rebuffed or scolded because it wasn't done "right" according to my standards?
- Have I employed passive-aggressive tactics in regard to housework in the past?
- Am I still being passive-aggressive?

These conversations can be scary to think about. That fear often prevents us from initiating a necessary talk, and keeps real progress from being made. What, specifically, are your fears or apprehensions about having this conversation?

PASSIVE-AGGRESSIVE BEHAVIOR

As tempting as passive-aggressive behavior can be, it doesn't work. When you reach a certain level of frustration, nothing seems more satisfying than releasing that tension one tersely worded note at a time. Unfortunately, it's counterproductive, petty, and only likely to result in defensiveness instead of changed behavior.

Instead of these behaviors:

- Leaving notes
- Slamming doors and drawers
- Piling someone's belongings on their bed or desk
- Going on "strike"
- Muttering under your breath

Try these:

- Having a conversation
- Asking for specific help
- Loosening your standards
- Developing a chore schedule (together)

What are some of your own passive-aggressive behaviors? (Be honest!)

....

....

....

What else can you do that's productive instead of passive-aggressive?

....

....

....

We dream of having a clean house—but who dreams of actually doing the cleaning?

—MARCUS BUCKINGHAM

MAKING A
FAIR CHORE CHART
PART 1

In a shared living situation, trying to divide tasks fairly can be fraught with drama. Finding an equitable way to split up the work can make the process much easier on everyone involved, and will almost definitely reduce the amount of bloodshed, tears, and rage smashing.

On the next page, list the tasks necessary to keep your household running, noting how long each task typically takes to complete and how often each needs to be repeated.

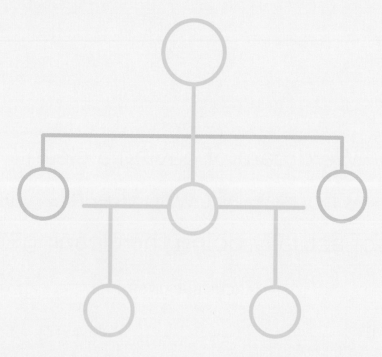

Task	How long	How often
Dishes		
Vacuuming/sweeping		
Grocery shopping		
Cooking meals		
Laundry		
Clean bathroom		
Take trash out		
Yard work		

MAKING A
FAIR CHORE CHART
PART 2

Now that you've listed the tasks it takes to keep your home running, it's time to figure out how you each feel about those tasks. In a shared living situation, it can be helpful to know who doesn't mind doing what task (and who really, really hates doing something). You can use this as a foundation for a more equitable division of chores. Fill out this chart to get started. Transfer your list of tasks from the previous page, then use your name or initials to mark off how you feel about each task

Task

Like it	Don't mind it	If I have to	Really hate it

MAKING A
FAIR CHORE CHART
PART 3

Now, using the information from the previous two charts, put together a chore chart that's equitable for everyone involved. Use factors like time investment (how long/how often) and emotional investment (like it/hate it—try to have an equal number of "hate it" tasks for each person, if necessary) to make it fair. If you switch off tasks, note which days/weeks each person is responsible for handling them.

Here's an example:

Task
Laundry
Dishes

How often	Who	Days/weeks
Weekly	Person A	Weeks 1 + 3
	Person B	Weeks 2 + 4
Daily	Person A	M, W, F, Sun
	Person B	T, Th, Sat

WHEN THINGS GO WRONG

Sometimes even the best-laid plans go a little awry. Try to come up with a plan if someone isn't respecting their part of the chart. If everyone involved is in agreement about what to do when things go wrong, it'll be easier to keep the peace and stay on track.

Write down your plan below and have everyone sign it.

My second-favorite
household chore is ironing.
My first being hitting
my head on the top bunk bed
until I faint.

—ERMA BOMBECK

TOOLS, TRACKERS, AND CHECKLISTS

Here's where you'll discover tools for:

- Supplies
- Time tracker
- Checklists

Keep yourself on track with the great progress you've already made with these lists and trackers. Use them to get started, follow along, or jump-start your momentum if you stall out.

BASIC SUPPLIES

These days, it's easy to be fooled into thinking you need a closetful of specialized cleaning products just to get and keep your home clean. If you went by ads and glossy home magazines, you'd think we all have to have dozens of different expensive products just to maintain a basic level of order.

Fortunately, you don't have to waste money on "must-haves"; you can keep a clean home with just a few cheap, easy basics:

- [ ] White vinegar
- [ ] Dish soap
- [ ] Baking soda
- [ ] Rags or cloths
- [ ] Broom/vacuum/mop
- [ ] Laundry detergent

And try this recipe for a great all-purpose cleaner: in an empty spray bottle, mix up a solution of half hot water, half white vinegar, and about a teaspoon of dish soap.

HABIT
TIMER

One of the reasons we put off doing tasks is because of how long we believe they're going to take. The truth is, though, they rarely take as long as we think they will, and we avoid doing pretty easy stuff because we have the wrong idea of how much time we'll need to invest. On the next page, make a list of your most dreaded regular tasks (emptying the dishwasher, changing your sheets, putting clean laundry away, etc.) and how long you think they'll each take. Then, do the task and time it, and record how long it actually took. Refer back to this page when you're dreading how long a task will take.

Dreaded task	How long I think it'll take	How long it actually took

HABIT
TRACKER

As you're trying to build habits, practicing accountability can be helpful. On the next page, list some of the habits you're trying to build. Each day, check off which tasks you've managed to do. This will give you an easy visual reference for where you're doing great and where you could use a little work.

Task	Monday	Tuesday	Wednesday
Make the bed			
Do the dishes			
Put clothes away			
Clear off table/counter			
Wipe down counters			

Thursday	Friday	Saturday	Sunday

GET
STARTED

If you're just beginning to get your mess under control and aren't quite at the level of needing detailed checklists just yet, here are a few tips to help you start tackling your chaos:

- **Start with the stuff that can stink.** That means that garbage, dirty dishes, and dirty laundry are always good places to begin.
- **Clean your working spaces early on.** Give yourself some space to use as you progress through your home.
- **Work from top to bottom.** Dust and dirt will fall as you work, so don't create extra steps for yourself.

- **When clearing off flat surfaces like counters, tables, or shelves, start with the biggest one.** It'll make the most visual impact, and also, everything else will seem easy in comparison.
- **Clean dry before you clean wet.** Dust before using cleaning products, and sweep before mopping.
- **Don't get bogged down with smaller, detailed projects** when you're doing a broad, overall cleanup. Make a note to come back to organizing the junk drawer or reshelving all of your books once you've completed your general cleaning. Getting stuck on insignificant tasks will ensure you waste all of your available time and energy on something that's not going to make a noticeable difference.

DAILY
CHECKLIST

Need a basic idea of what to do every day to keep ahead of the mess? Here are some general suggestions for daily tasks. Add anything else that applies to your everyday life.

- [ ] Make your bed.
- [ ] Wash the dishes.
- [ ] Put your clothes and shoes away.
- [ ] Deal with all incoming mail.
- [ ] Wipe down kitchen and bathroom counters.
- [ ] Clean the litter box (if applicable).
- [ ] Do one or two 20/10s in an area that needs it.
- [ ] ....
- [ ] ....
- [ ] ....
- [ ] ....
- [ ] ....
- [ ] ....

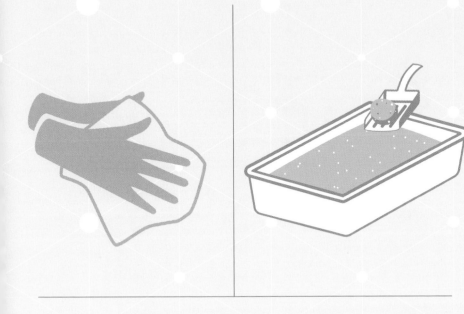

WEEKLY CHECKLIST

Once a week, go a little more in-depth with your cleaning. Keep in mind that you don't have to do everything on the checklist at once; you can spread it out over the course of the week.

- [ ] Wash the sheets.
- [ ] Vacuum/mop/sweep all floors.
- [ ] Wash, dry, and put away laundry.
- [ ] Wipe down the stovetop and oven door.
- [ ] Clean the toilet.
- [ ] Clean the shower/bathtub.
- [ ] Take the trash out.
- [ ] Wash all the towels.
- [ ] Put away everything on bedroom floor.
- [ ] Put away everything in common areas.
- [ ] ....
- [ ] ....
- [ ] ....
- [ ] ....
- [ ] ....
- [ ] ....

MONTHLY CHECKLIST

Every month, make an effort to complete each of these tasks. Don't try to do them all at once. It's much easier to just do one every few days or so.

- ☐ Dust all surfaces.
- ☐ Wipe down or vacuum the baseboards.
- ☐ Clean out the refrigerator.
- ☐ Wipe down the bathroom walls.
- ☐ Clean light switches and door handles.
- ☐ Throw away old magazines, shred or file old bills and mail.
- ☐ Clean out and organize the pantry.
- ☐ Vacuum your mattress.
- ☐ ....
- ☐ ....
- ☐ ....
- ☐ ....
- ☐ ....
- ☐ ....

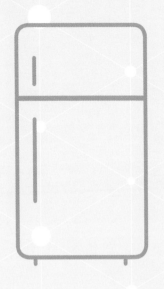

SEASONAL CHECKLIST

A change of seasons is a great time to do those things that need to be looked after only a few times a year. Forget "spring cleaning"; keep on track all year long with just a little extra effort.

- [ ] Wash the curtains/clean vertical blinds.
- [ ] Sort through clothes; donate/repair as needed.
- [ ] Vacuum/clean upholstered furniture.
- [ ] Clean the oven.
- [ ] Clean out bathroom drawers and cabinets.
- [ ] Rotate the mattress.
- [ ] ....
- [ ] ....
- [ ] ....
- [ ] ....
- [ ] ....
- [ ] ....

ROOM-BY-ROOM
CLEANING CHECKLISTS

Need to clean a specific room, but you just can't figure out how? There's no shame in that! Here, find some basic checklists for cleaning different rooms. You may need to add or get rid of tasks on these lists, depending on your home and what's in it, but you can always use these as a good foundation to get started.

BATHROOM CLEANING
CHECKLIST

- [ ] Put items on counters/shelves away where they belong.
- [ ] Spray the shower walls and tub with cleaner.
- [ ] Put cleaner in the toilet bowl.
- [ ] Wipe/scrub shower/tub walls, under bottles, and around faucets. Rinse.
- [ ] Scrub the toilet bowl.
- [ ] Wipe down the toilet seat and surfaces.
- [ ] Clean/wipe down the exhaust fan and light fixtures.
- [ ] Clean around the faucets and drains.
- [ ] Dust the shelves and fixtures.
- [ ] Clean and wipe out the sink.
- [ ] Wipe down the countertops.
- [ ] Clean the mirror(s).
- [ ] Sweep and mop the floor.

KITCHEN CLEANING
CHECKLIST

- [ ] Fill the sink with hot, soapy water.
- [ ] Collect the dishes and bring them to the sink to soak.
- [ ] Starting with the most cluttered counter, clear flat surfaces.
- [ ] Wipe down the countertops.
- [ ] Wipe down all appliances.
- [ ] Clean inside the microwave.*
- [ ] Clean the stovetop.
- [ ] Clean the windows.
- [ ] Wash all dishes or load dishwasher.
- [ ] Replace sponges, dishcloths, and towels.
- [ ] Sweep and mop the floor.

*TIP: Microwave a bowl of water with some citrus or vinegar for several minutes. Let the steam loosen cooked-on crud in the microwave before you wipe it down.

LESS OFTEN:

- ☐ Clean out fridge, removing expired items and wiping down shelves and drawers.
- ☐ Clean out and organize the pantry or cabinets.
- ☐ Wipe down the cabinet fronts.
- ☐ Clean the oven hood.
- ☐ Organize under the sink.
- ☐ Clean the dishwasher filter.
- ☐ Dust the light fixtures.
- ☐ Clean under the refrigerator and stove.

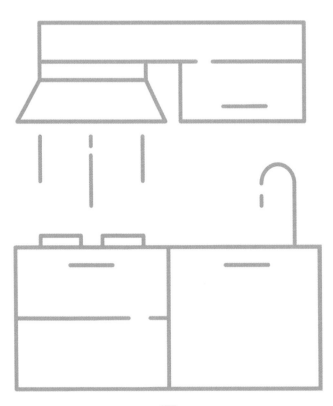

BEDROOM CLEANING
CHECKLIST

- ☐ Collect the trash and dishes and bring them to the appropriate place.
- ☐ Collect the dirty laundry in hamper or laundry basket.
- ☐ Put clean clothes away.
- ☐ Put shoes/other accessories away.
- ☐ Clear off flat surfaces (dresser, nightstand, etc.).
- ☐ Dust surfaces, light fixtures, baseboards, etc.

- [ ] Clean the windows.
- [ ] Put away anything remaining on the floor, bed, chair, or elsewhere.
- [ ] Wash the sheets/bedding.
- [ ] Make your bed.
- [ ] Vacuum or sweep the floor.

BASIC CLEANING CHECKLIST FOR ALMOST ANY ROOM

- [ ] Collect any obvious trash or recycling and dispose of it.
- [ ] Collect laundry and/or dishes and put them where they belong.
- [ ] Start with the largest flat surface (table, counter, dresser top, shelf, etc.). Sort, clear, put away items, throw away/recycle if needed, and wipe down.
- [ ] Repeat on all flat surfaces.
- [ ] Pick up everything off the floor and put items away.
- [ ] Dust anything that needs dusting, working from top to bottom.
- [ ] Vacuum or sweep and mop the floor.

Bedroom

Bathroom

Kitchen

Living Room

Dining Room

Misc.

YOU DID IT!

Now that you've come to the end of this journal, think about where you started, where you are now, and everything you've done in between. When you started this journal and this journey, you gave yourself a goal for your ideal home. Whether that was having friends over, hosting a dinner or a holiday, or just being able to relax with the things that make you comfortable and happy, hopefully you've either achieved that goal or have come far closer to it than you thought you could.

Remember, keeping your home clean and comfortable is an ongoing project. You'll have times when you're very successful, and times when you let things fall to the wayside. Just keep in mind that you can start over again at any time.

Be kind to yourself,
learn to love your home,
and go forth and unfuck
your habitat!

NOTES

ABOUT THE AUTHOR

RACHEL HOFFMAN launched Unf*ck Your Habitat in 2011 to motivate regular people to get up, start cleaning, and get their lives in order. Her advice has appeared in publications and on websites such as *Glamour*, *Elle*, *Real Simple*, NBC News, Apartment Therapy, Livestrong, *House Beautiful*, *The Times* (London), Quick and Dirty Tips, Ravishly, and Lifehacker. She lives in New England with her husband and two Chihuahuas.